Old Cuminestown, Garmond and Ne

Douglas G. Lockhart

CW00601644

Castle of Auchry is a farm one and a half miles north-west of Cuminestown. Until 1875 it was owned by the Earl of Fife, one of North East Scotland's largest landowners. In the 1870s he began to sell parts of his extensive estates, and the lands known as Cairnhill were purchased by one of his estate managers, John Hannay. When Hannay moved away from the area he sold Castle of Auchry in 1891 to the sitting tenant, George Forrest. In the middle distance mainly hidden by trees is Aulton Cottage (page 5) while the road leads to the Bridge of Pot (page 6) and Cuminestown.

1

© Douglas G. Lockhart, 2015
First published in the United Kingdom, 2015,
by Stenlake Publishing Ltd.
www.stenlake.co.uk
ISBN 9781840337181

The publishers regret that they cannot supply
copies of any pictures featured in this book.

In New Byth, James Urquhart made plans to develop linen weaving and established a company with capital from merchants in Banff and Edinburgh. Two notices in the *Aberdeen Journal* in 1771 and 1772 advertised cloth and offered employment to weavers for twelve months. The company specialised in coarse cloth in the Osnaburg style and some of the output was exported to the West Indies possibly to become clothing for slaves on the plantations. Linen weaving was an unstable occupation and whilst it may have been attractive to work from home, fluctuations in demand, volatility in the price and supply of flax and in the late eighteenth century competition from cotton were major difficulties for the workforce. The building in the foreground was a linen weaving shop and is now divided into cottages.

Acknowledgements

I would like to thank the staffs of Aberdeen City Libraries, Aberdeenshire Archives, Old Aberdeen, National Library of Scotland, Edinburgh, National Records of Scotland, Edinburgh, and Carnegie Library, Ayr, for their help with my enquiries. I am grateful to Alexander Jamieson, Geoff Marston, Marie Milne, Susan McRae, Alistair Strachan and Diana Webster. Newspaper advertisements on the inside back cover have been reproduced with the permission of Aberdeen City Libraries.

Further Reading

The websites and books listed below were used by the author during his research. None of the books are available from Stenlake Publishing. Those interested in finding out more are advised to contact Aberdeen Central Library and the National Library of Scotland, Edinburgh, which have comprehensive collections of local history books, maps and newspapers including the *Aberdeen Journal*, *Banffshire Journal*, *Buchan Observer* and the *Turriff Advertiser*.

Duffus, H.G. and S.H., *A History of Monquhitter*, Meigle Printers, Galashiels, 1985.

Godsman, J., *King Edward, Aberdeenshire*, Banffshire Journal Limited, Banff, 1952.

Hamilton, H. (ed.), *The County of Aberdeen, The Third Statistical Account of Scotland*, Vol. 7, Collins, Glasgow, 1960.

Lockhart, D.G., 'The planned villages of Buchan, 1750–1900', *Transactions of the Buchan Field Club*, XVIII (Part III), 1979, pp. 40–51.

Lockhart, D.G., *Scottish Planned Villages*, Scottish History Society, Edinburgh, 2012.

Moir, J., *A New History of Buchan from the Earliest Times to the Present Day*, Peterhead Sentinel, 1896–98.

McWilliam, Rev. T., *Sketch of a Quiet Buchan Parish*, Banffshire Journal Office, Banff, 1899.

McWilliam, Rev. T., *The Kirks of the Turriff Presbytery*, Banffshire Journal Office, Banff, 1904.

Paterson, A., *Memories of Monquhitter or Reminiscences of the early 40s*, Banffshire Journal Office, Banff, 1901.

Pratt, Rev. J.B., *Buchan*, Heritage Press reprint, Turriff, 1981.

Robertson, J. Minto (ed.), *The War Book of Turriff and Twelve Miles Round: A Memorial 1914–1919*, The Turriff and District Ex-Service Men's Association, 1926.

Smith, A., *A New History of Aberdeenshire*, 2 vols., L. Smith, Aberdeen, 1875.

Withrington, D. (ed.), *The Statistical Account of Scotland 1791–1799 edited by Sir John Sinclair, Volume XV: North and East Aberdeenshire*, EP Publishing Limited reprint, Wakefield, 1982.

The *New Statistical Account of Scotland*, Vol. 12: Aberdeen (1845): www.electricscotland.com/history/statistical/volume12.html

Ordnance Survey maps provided by the National Library of Scotland: www.maps.nls.uk/os/index.html

Introduction

The three villages in this book are located in north-west Aberdeenshire with Turriff, the nearest town, around six miles from Cuminestown. Several villages in this area such as Strichen, New Aberdour and Mintlaw have already featured in books published by Stenlake Publishing. These villages were founded by local landowners in the late eighteenth and early nineteenth century when restructuring of farms and fields and other agricultural improvements took place. Agricultural labourers, cottars and tradesmen were rehoused in the new planned villages and investment by landowners and merchants in small-scale textile industries provided employment for spinners and weavers.

David Knox was born at Bodiechell in Fyvie Parish in 1850. He served his apprenticeship at Stanryknowe (page 30 and the back cover) and for a time worked in Peterhead and Glasgow as a clothier. In 1877 he took over the tenancy of the merchant's shop in the Low Square, Cuminestown. His business also included the sale of farm and garden seeds, ironmongery and tailoring, and was very successful, enabling him to buy the feu. The shop was described in 1929 as 'substantial, up-to-date, and in excellent order' when it was sold. The new owner, William Mair, remained a familiar name in the village for many years, however in 1967 Philip Watt, an hotelier in Muir of Ord, Ross-shire, took over the post office that had previously been at the Tennant's shop and combined this with the merchandise business at Mair's premises. Today, the convenience store is the last shop open in the three villages.

Cuminestown and New Byth were among the earliest examples of planned villages in the district and date from the 1760s while Garmond was founded towards the end of the eighteenth century, with the first baptism recorded there in April 1800. Since many villages were established at this time, it is probably not surprising that none grew to become small towns; the villages in this book recorded their greatest combined population of only 1,450 at the 1871 Census.

Cuminestown was founded in 1761 by Joseph Cumine of Auchry, a leading agriculturalist whose friends included Sir Archibald Grant of Monymusk who planned Archiestown (Moray) in the same year. An advertisement in the *Aberdeen Journal* on 7 December 1761 announced that 'All Merchants, Tradesmen and others who incline Feus in the Kirktown of Montwhiter may apply to the Proprietor ...'. The village consisted of two streets, one on a north-south axis later named Main Street, which incorporated Low Square and was situated a short distance from the parish church. A second, longer, street was laid out in an east-west direction and became known as High Street. A feature of the early villages were attempts by landowners to develop the linen industry. A manufacturing company was established to produce cloth and trysts (markets) were established for the sale of animals, merchant goods and linen cloth and yarn. Lastly, fields in the neighbourhood were divided into lots measuring one to two and a half acres, which provided keep for a cow. There is a glowing tribute to Joseph Cumine's project in the *Statistical Account of Scotland*: 'Settlers annually flocked to Cuminestown ... and the village, built of freestone, soon assumed a flourishing appearance'. Although the linen industry was short lived, markets were held in the village and it became home to tradesmen such as tailors, shoemakers and weavers and there were several merchant's shops.

New Byth, built on the ridge of a hill, dates from 1763 and its founder, James Urquhart of Byth, was much influenced by developments taking place just two and a half miles away in Cuminestown. Tradesmen, a small-scale linen industry, agricultural labourers and part-time farming on the village lands once again were the characteristic features of the village. Finally, Garmond was built on both sides of a minor road to the east of the Auchry House policies. Several of its tradesmen were tailors and shoemakers, trades that would continue into the twentieth century; many however were handloom weavers, stocking knitters and agricultural labourers who would face declining work opportunities from the mid-nineteenth century onwards. New Byth and Garmond suffered from rapid depopulation after the 1871 Census. Losses were soon being noticed; the *Banffshire Journal* on 22 June 1880 reported that the 'population of the village and estate of Byth is at the present time considerably on the wane … leaving many subjects untenanted'. Cuminestown however had a broader range of employment and its location on the road between Turriff, New Deer and Maud, which was the junction for the railway lines to Peterhead and Fraserburgh from Aberdeen from 1865, helped sustain more shops and businesses such as bakeries and carriers.

By 1971, the combined population of the three villages had dwindled to around 600 and those of working age who remained were on the whole more mobile and could access facilities in towns such as Turriff and Banff or travel to Aberdeen. All the villages have suffered from the closure of what were once considered important services. In the early 1960s the shop and the primary school in Garmond both shut and there was a procession of shop closures in New Byth from the early 1960s onwards and more recently the church, primary school, hotel and several voluntary organizations have all ceased to exist. In 1969 Cuminestown had nine shops, a bank, post office and a police station, and many of these can be found among the photographs in this book. In an era of growing car ownership it was not surprising that small shops were unable to compete with supermarkets and when local shops closed down the impact tended to disadvantage poorer and elderly residents who felt increasingly isolated. However, all sections of the community were dismayed when regional and national organisations such as Grampian Police, the Clydesdale Bank and the Post Office proposed the closure of their village offices. In Cuminestown today there is just one shop and a hairdresser, and the Church of Scotland now welcomes communicants from New Byth. However, the long-established Commercial Hotel remains open, as does the primary school, while a biscuit factory maintains the village's bakery traditions. Post office counter services ended in 2009 and have been replaced by a mobile post office that visits the village on weekdays. Auchry House, the centrepiece of Joseph Cumine's redesigned landscape, was an earlier casualty, having been demolished following its purchase in 1966 by a dairy farmer from Macduff.

Readers who enjoy exploring historic landscapes should consult the Ordnance Survey 1:25000 map [Sheet 426: Banff, Macduff & Turriff] which gives a good indication of what is on offer here. The photographs in this book are arranged to form a tour of the landscape, beginning on the western outskirts of Cuminestown and skirting the former policies of Auchry House. Cuminestown is next explored and then we head for Garmond. From East Garmond Farm we descend to the watercourse of the Burn of Monquhitter, where there were several meal mills, before regaining higher ground at New Byth.

This view of the southern approach to New Byth was taken in the late 1930s. The main change is the demolition, around 1934, of the old distillery store on the west side of Bridge Street to make way for three blocks of social housing (Bridge Terrace). Two semi-detached single-storey houses also built by the county council about the same time can be seen on the edge of the lotted lands. Even so there was dissatisfaction in the mid 1950s with the quality and availability of housing and a petition signed by 246 residents was presented to the Aberdeenshire Housing Committee. The county sanitary inspector countered by stating that there was no demand for new housing, six existing properties could be brought up to an acceptable standard and that 'twenty houses were in a ruinous and dilapidated condition, and should be removed immediately and the sites cleared up'. It was another four years before more council housing would be built, this time in Main Street.

The ford on the Burn of Monquhitter is less than a mile west of Cuminestown on a minor road off the B9170. In the background of this charming scene is Aulton Cottage, Honeynook, which was owned between 1887 and 1949 by the Tennant family, general merchants. Their neighbour Peter Smart Cowie (1858–1919), farmer at Netherton, Delgaty, who was related to the Tennant family by marriage, can be seen watering his horses while on his way to the smiddy. Peter Cowie had served an apprenticeship at the Tennant's business but he turned to farming at Netherton when his father removed to the larger farm of Easter Bo. Today, a footbridge still crosses the stream but the ford has gone and a large storage shed has been erected on the far bank.

The Bridge of Pot which carries the road to Turriff over the Burn of Monquhitter was rebuilt at the beginning of the twentieth century. It was officially opened on 14 September 1901 by John Runcieman (1831–1915), farmer at Auchmill, King Edward. In doing so he paid tribute to the skills of the contractor, James Ferguson (1852–1913), mason and farmer at Bogtama near Fyvie, whose impressive portfolio included the chapel at Haddo House and the bridge over the Ythan at Lewes of Fyvie. The ceremony was well attended and among those present were local farmers, the parish minister, the Turriff postmaster and several of the oldest residents of the district. The correspondent of the *Buchan Observer* reported it 'a compact and pleasing structure, making a marked addition to the amenities of the already picturesque hollow of Mill of Pot'. The bridge decking was replaced in 1995 after a survey found that it would be unable to withstand increases in permitted vehicle weights.

Entrance to Auchry House, Cuminestown.

Built by Joseph Cumine in 1767 on the gently sloping ground on the opposite side of the valley from Cuminestown, Auchry House was constructed using the local red sandstone. About fifteen years later Francis Douglas made a diversion there during his tour of the east coast. He noted that the house 'is surrounded by a broad belt of planting, not of one, but almost every kind of timber that had been planted in Britain … The house and garden stand on an eminence, about the middle of the farm and overlook the rivulet, which has a wooden bridge thrown over it, leading to Monquhitter, now Cuminestown a fine village lately erected by Mr Cumine'. The west gate lodge has stood guard on the north side of the Bridge of Pot since it was built in 1830, about the time Cumine's son, Archibald, sold the estate.

AUCHRY HOUSE MONQUHITTER

In 1830 much of the Auchry estate became the property of the Lumsden family; however, towards the close of the century Auchry's owner Richard Lumsden was an absentee living in Bridge of Allan near Stirling. Gradually parts of the estate were sold off while the village feu duties were sold to George Wood, a Turriff solicitor. Auchry changed hands again in 1966 when it was purchased by James Robertson of Souter Street Dairy in Macduff. He demolished the old house, an event described in *Milk News* in September 1968: 'The new "mansion" of Auchry … is a building – 140 ft. by 80 ft. by 20 ft. … the home, in fact, of the 100-plus Friesian herd run by the new owner of Auchry Home Farm …'. A Cumine family crest made from the local red sandstone is now incorporated into the garden wall of a new bungalow built by Robertson. It is the only surviving feature of Auchry House visible today.

A lawn lay in front of Auchry House and to the east was a lake, formed out of two small fields that had originally been reclaimed from the swampy ground. To provide employment, Cumine had workmen build embankments and a channel was cut from the watercourse of the Burn of Monquhitter near Waulkmill to feed the water which formed the lake. The lake and its wooded islets survived the many changes to the Auchry estate and the only significant development has been the construction of a large bungalow and separate garage building on the northern bank.

Writing in the late 1890s, James Moir noted that in the Parish of Monquhitter, 'Even in the best parts … it looks as if man were at war with stubborn nature, and getting the worst of it. The only locality where he seems to have gained a victory is in the neighbourhood of the House of Auchry, where considerable plantations … break the dismal monotony by their verdure and variety of colouring'. This view of the western approach to Auchry House, flanked by thick belts of mature shelter trees and hawthorn hedges, would have met with approval from Moir. Auchry was much admired by visitors and the policies were a popular venue for school and church summer picnics. In the 1880s the Garmond Games took place on the green.

The waterfall was located at the south-west corner of the lake with the water going back into the main watercourse that runs in an east–west direction on the edge of the policies. It is marked as a sluice on the 25-inch-to-a-mile Ordnance Survey map [Aberdeenshire Sheet XII.9] which was surveyed in 1870. Sadly this attractive feature is no more; the banking has been built up and a large diameter pipe now takes surplus water away.

Gammie, Photo, Turriff.

The Ladies Bridge and ford across the Burn of Monquhitter was located only a few yards downstream from the waterfall. It provided a direct route between Auchry House and the village via Chapel Brae and St Luke's Square. The wooden bridge with its stone steps on both sides and the ford are still both there today.

Parish Church, Cuminestown.

Gammie, Photo.

The Parish Church of Monquhitter, which was built in 1764, was described in the *New Statistical Account* 'as being in considerable disrepair'. The foundation stone of a new church was laid on 28 June 1867 and it opened a year later. In recent times dwindling church rolls have resulted in parishioners from New Byth attending Monquhitter church and in 2003 the ministry was linked with St Andrew's Church in Turriff. The tall memorial stone in the centre of the photograph commemorates Thomas Ferrier, a much respected local doctor who took up an appointment in Accra in West Africa in 1890 and died at sea off Freetown on his way home on 13 June 1893, and also his widow, Jane Booth of Parkhill House and her aunt and uncle.

The earliest map which shows the hotel buildings was George Campbell Smith's survey of Auchry Estate in 1830. Early in the twentieth century an advertisement for the hotel in *Macdonald's Scottish Directory* offered 'every comfort and convenience for commercial gentlemen'. The modern history of the hotel is synonymous with the Robertson family who invested heavily in the building. William Robertson senior (1905–89), who had been a farmer at Hillhead of Tyrie, purchased the hotel in 1959 and spent £5,000 improving the hotel. A large function suite was added by his son and the *Turriff Advertiser* on 6 June 1980 reported that 300 people were present at the official opening by District Councillor John Gordon.

The shop in this photograph was owned for 45 years by George Fordyce (1836–1924) who was a shoemaker by trade. He diversified his interests and opened a merchant's shop, and also dealt in seeds, feeding stuffs and manures. In addition Fordyce supplemented his income by cultivating a large area of lotted lands in the vicinity of the village. Adam Cooper was the son of Jean, George Fordyce's sister, and lived with George's family in Cuminestown before marrying. He served his apprenticeship as a tailor at Millbrex in neighbouring Fyvie Parish. Cooper was in charge of the merchant's shop owned by Fordyce between 1888 and 1908. The tailoring trade at this time was still thriving and there was sufficient business to support an apprentice. Although Cooper was well integrated into local social life – he was active in the church and the Lodge of Oddfellows – as with many other people in the North East at that time, the prospects offered by a new life abroad proved irresistible and he left for Australia along with his wife and two children in 1909. The shop premises and the adjoining house which fronted on to Auchry Road were purchased in 1977 by Grampian Regional Council who demolished the buildings two years later to make way for road widening and landscaping.

Cuminestown and Garmond at the end of the nineteenth century were well-known for their shoemakers and tailors. As depopulation gathered momentum shoemakers, who were already under pressure from factory-made footwear, had fewer customers. James Burr, possibly noticing a diminishing trade, gave up his shop in the Low Square and moved to Ellon in 1898 where he became a boot and shoe traveller. However, another boot and shoe shop on the north-east corner of Low Square (12 Main Street) owned by Alexander Cockburn (1879–1923), son of James Cockburn, tailor, Waterloo Cottage, Garmond, survived for longer. Cockburn was also a typical feuar who, in addition to his trade, farmed part of the village lands; such was his success in farming that he acquired the farm of Braeside of Middlehill. After his death his widow ran a drapery and shoe shop until selling up in 1930. At the beginning of the twentieth century there were two bakeries in Main Street. The Central Bakery was in the Low Square (31/33 Main Street) and had been built in 1888 for John Rennie. A succession of bakers worked here until it was purchased in 1925 by Charlotte Douglas whose husband James (1892–1971) was a master baker in Montrose. He established an oatcake factory in Cuminestown and a bakery in Laurencekirk (Kincardineshire). His Howe o' the Mearns oatcakes became famous and the business became known as Howe o' the Mearns Ltd. He was succeeded by his son and son-in-law who sold the bakery in 1981 to Gerald McKenzie of Turriff. Today it is known as 'Mr McKenzie's Biscuits'.

This photograph of the police station in Main Street was taken shortly before it closed in 1993. The police force had carried out a review of policing and it was decided to close a number of village stations, with officers concentrated in the larger offices such as the one at Turriff. The community council was not impressed and its chairman, Harold Cormack, noted that, 'It is a regrettable sign of the times that financial constraints are more important than a community'. At a public consultation in the village, speaker after speaker stressed the importance of having a local bobby who 'knew his way around the district and knew the people'. Nevertheless the closure went ahead and the former station is now a private house.

Main Street, Cuminestown.

Gammie, Photo.

James Tennant was born at Teuchar on the outskirts of Cuminestown in 1841 and in 1860 he succeeded his uncle in a successful merchant's business in the Low Square. In 1876 he moved to this shop at the junction of Main Street and High Street, though it was not until 1895 that he purchased the property. He was much involved in community affairs as a justice of the peace, an elder in the United Free Church, and as a member of the parochial board and the parish council. On his death in 1909 he left a fund to construct playing fields in the village and these were officially opened by Robert Boothby MP in July 1933. His son, William John Tennant (1877–1951), succeeded him in the business. The adjacent building was the first Episcopal Chapel, built in 1792 and superseded by St Luke's Church in 1844.

The staff of James Tennant's shop often posed for photographs by William Gammie of Turriff, including this one taken about 1910. The tall gentleman wearing a bespoke suit is Robert Anderson, the shop tailor. In its later years the main shop was run by Ethel Russell, eldest daughter of W.J. Tennant and last member of the family living in Cuminestown. She retired in 1975, a year before her death. The small annexe to the right of the shop became the post office shortly before the First World War, when it replaced the office at 'Willowbank' on the High Street (page 25). The post office moved only once more, in 1967, to Phillip Watt's shop (Mair's) in Low Square. The shop remains open as a Costcutter although post office services ended in 2009.

Following the retirement of Mrs Russell, the Tennant family shop and warehouse were sold to Aberdeenshire Junior League team Cuminestown Football Club to be converted into a social club. The official opening took place on 28 April 1976 and was performed by Joe Harper who played for Aberdeen F.C. The Clydesdale Bank branch, which first occupied this site as the Town and County Bank in 1893, was still open for business when this photograph was taken in 1984. However, the withdrawal of the Clydesdale Bank from villages throughout Aberdeenshire meant that the Cuminestown branch served its last customers in October 1992. The bank house was advertised for sale the following May and was sold a few months later. The football social club closed down about eight years ago and at the time of writing was being advertised for sale by estate agents in Turriff.

Cuminestown, Looking up.

Gammie, Photo.

This photograph was taken from opposite the brewery on Teuchar Road and looks towards High Street, which gradually climbs towards Waggle Hill on the outskirts of the village. In the foreground on the left are the buildings at the rear of Tennant's shop and beyond is the gable of Bank House at 'The Corner'. The detached house partly hidden by the tree on the right is 'Clevedon', which was built for Dr William Leighton Ross in 1894. When he left to work in Edinburgh it was let for a few years to another doctor, Hugh McGregor Forbes, and in 1906 the house was purchased by James Tennant. It remained in the ownership of the Tennant family until 1977.

19

CUMINESTOWN SCHOOL.

Gairmie. Photo.

James Duncan (1828–1907) established an architect's practice in Turriff in 1862 and one of his earliest projects was Cuminestown school house. Duncan quickly established a reputation for designing public buildings, so it came as no surprise when he was appointed architect to the Monquhitter School Board. In the late 1890s and in 1905 the practice was employed to draw plans for an extension and other alterations to the school buildings. The Victorian and Edwardian complex remained in use until 1964 when a new school was built off Thornhill Road. The old school was demolished in 1972 and sheltered accommodation for the elderly, known as 'Cumrye', was built on the site in 1975. The old school bell can still be seen on the gable of one of the buildings.

After the Second World War there were around 170 pupils and a staff of a dozen teachers some of whom worked part-time. When this photograph was taken at the time of the Coronation in June 1953, Stephen West (seated centre) had just succeeded James B. Calder as headmaster and he and Francis Hay (standing left) taught the secondary pupils. John Brown (standing right) was responsible for technical subjects while there were four or sometimes five full-time teachers in the infant and primary departments and four domestic staff. In addition, visiting teachers took classes in music, physical education, domestic science and art. Francis Hay and John Brown later taught at Turriff Academy and Stephen West retired in 1964.

In April 1957, 36 pupils in the three secondary classes attended Monquhitter School. Responsibility for much of the teaching was divided between Stephen West (mathematics, science and religious studies) and Francis Hay (English, biology and hobbies). The new school, which was officially opened on 22 October 1964 by Alexander L. Young, County Director of Education, also had a secondary department. However, only six years later falling rolls led to these classes being transferred to Turriff Academy. The impending closure drew a withering response from the Turriff Education Committee which complained of a waste of public money and poor educational planning. Today, the primary school continues to occupy the extensive buildings in Cuminestown.

The brewery farm on the south side of Teuchar Road probably dates from the early nineteenth century. At the end of the century the tenant was Alexander Fraser who also had an aerated water factory in Turriff. The upper level of the building was occasionally used for dances and other social functions and the last dance held there marked Edward VII's coronation in 1902. After Fraser's death in 1903, his widow carried on the business for a few years. Brewing was discontinued around 1908 when Adam Beaton took up the tenancy and afterwards supplies were received in bulk and bottled and sold on the premises. Beaton was also a carrier who had previously lived in New Byth and Aberdeen. When Beaton retired in 1933, the business was sold to the firm of Alexander and Keith (later A. & J. Keith) which expanded to become a major local employer in the post-war period. When a dinner was held at the Commercial Hotel in November 1958 to celebrate their 25th birthday the fleet numbered eleven vehicles and the firm employed fifteen men.

CUMINESTOWN· HIGH STREET.

GAMMIE. PHOTO.

The building with the canopy over the pavement at 12 High Street housed the Porter Bakery and shop. The origins of the Porter Bakery can be traced back to 1832 when it was founded by Alexander Porter (1809–96). Porter became the village bank agent in 1876 and his son took over the bakery. The business remained in family ownership until 1978 and today the factory is still in use though the retail shop has closed. Although no motor vehicles are to be seen in the photograph, there is a petrol pump at the bakery and further up the street there was a large garage belonging to the haulage firm, Alexander and Keith.

This photograph appears on a postcard postmarked 1903 and covers the area to the east of the Porter Bakery as far as the large tree next to St Luke's Church (page 28). The landscape consists mainly of single-storey cottages, several of which are still thatched. Many of the older and unimproved properties were rented from the estate and on some feus there were back cottages as well, out of sight of the photographer, which provided cheap housing for poor people. Few two-storey houses are in this view: 'Willowbank', which housed the post office, is on the right (page 25) and the two on the left are the only plots to have been redeveloped.

HIGH STREET, Cuminestown.

Gammie, Photo.

Postal services in Cuminestown during the second half of the nineteenth century were associated with the Lamb family. John Lamb (1828–93) was a carpenter who became one of the pillars of the community and at the time of his death held the offices of postmaster, school board clerk, assistant registrar and elder in the parish church. He never married and lived with his sisters Jane and Isabella at 62 High Street, a short distance from St Luke's Church. After Lamb's death, postal services moved to the house closest to the camera, 19 High Street, 'Willowbank', which was owned for a time by William Jaffray who married Lucy Jane Lamb, John Lamb's niece and postmistress in 1899.

Pictured in front of their house at 42 High Street, Cuminestown, in 1909 are Alexander Cockburn (1853–1932) and his second wife, Maggie Ann Joss (1858–1932). He was the son of Alexander Cockburn of Corbshill, New Deer, and Helen Trail of Pitullie, and became a farm servant who like many workers at the time often moved at 'term days' at Whitsunday and Martinmas. After his first wife (Margaret Smith) died, Cockburn settled in Aberdeen where he worked as a carter. He moved again to Cuminestown in 1906, after he had inherited a house owned by his father, and remarried. Cockburn sadly collapsed and died moments before the start of harvest thanksgiving at Monquhitter Church, resulting in the cancellation of the service. His house was a typical Victorian property with the Cockburn family living in one half and the other occupied by two tenants. Each semi-detached house consisted of two rooms on the ground floor and another two rooms upstairs. A later owner, William Strachan, farmer, Millfield, named it Edon House, the name it still has today.

This photograph shows features that were new to Cuminestown in the inter-war period. In the middle distance is the garage opened in 1928 by Andrew Scott, son of a local dairy farmer, who had previously had a small plumbing and cycle repair business. The garage was the only one in the village during the next 40 years. After his death in 1970, the business was continued by his sons until 1988 when it was acquired by Roy Allan Cameron of Boyndlie near Fraserburgh. Cameron Motors, which later became Cameron Autotech, purchased the A. & J. Keith haulage contractors premises at 23 High Street in 2004 and have developed a car servicing and MOT testing facility. The former Scott garage is now in a semi-derelict condition and is currently used to store building materials. Closer to the camera are two blocks of semi-detached houses that were the earliest social housing in the village when built by the county council in 1934.

ST. LUKE'S CHURCH, MONQUHITTER

The first Episcopal chapel dates from 1792 and was in Main Street (page 16). In 1844 a new church was consecrated on the north side of the Square on High Street, a site that had been common land where the village cows grazed. A rectory and church hall were also built on the feu. The Episcopal Church flourished in Victorian and Edwardian times with its congregation drawn from land-owning families, farmers and those who disliked the strict orthodoxy of the established church. The break-up and sale of many landed estates after the First World War impacted on the fortunes of the congregation. In the late 1950s St Luke's ceased to have a resident rector and instead pastoral care was provided from Turriff. The parsonage was rented before eventually being sold and the purchaser, ironically, was a retired Church of Scotland minister.

Left: The small square on the High Street became known as St Luke's Square after the Episcopal chapel was built. The houses are mainly small single-storey cottages that were rented to farm workers, widows and spinsters. In contrast, there are only two owner-occupied houses in the photograph. The large two-storey house on the west edge of the Square was owned by Isabella Gerrard, the youngest daughter of a Turriff watchmaker and the other was the home of James Callum, horse hirer and bus owner, a younger brother of William Callum who was innkeeper at the Commercial Hotel between 1901 and 1919.

Right: The Episcopal school house, the more distant of the two houses on the right set back from the street, closed in the late 1870s. This was purchased in 1897 by Thomas Chaddock, a coastguard's son. In early life he had gone to sea, but between 1889 and 1897 he owned the store at Stanryknowe (page 30). Chaddock named his new property Anchor Cottage. However, the lure of a maritime life proved too strong and he moved to Aberdeen, becoming a boat builder while Anchor Cottage was occupied by tenants. He returned to Cuminestown in 1916 and three years later, James Christie, a shoemaker who had served with the Gordon Highlanders in the First World War, took over the tenancy. Known locally as 'The Sooter' [sic], he purchased Anchor Cottage in 1925, however his health had been affected by war wounds and he died in 1941, aged 47. His wife and son carried on the footwear shop for a few years before Anchor Cottage was sold to one of his apprentices, Charles Wilson (1913–99), who was the last shoemaker living and working in Cuminestown.

STANRYKNOWE & AUCHRY.

Gammie, Photo.

The shop was purchased from Leitch's trustees in 1911 by John Duguid (1879–1930), a tailor who was born in Garmond and had worked in Tarves and Aberdeen. His ownership coincided with difficult trading conditions during the First World War as well as the years leading up to the Great Depression. Following his death the business was sold to James Jamieson and the family continued to run a licensed grocer's until 1989. When this author visited in February 2015, the shop premises were unoccupied and in the early stages of renovation. The field opposite now contains local authority housing built in the late 1940s.

Garmond was founded in the late 1790s. It is not mentioned in the *Statistical Account* of Monquhitter Parish which was published in 1791–92 and the earliest entries in the Register of Baptisms occur in 1800 and 1801. The village consists of a long street on higher ground east of the policies that surrounded Auchry House. Garmond was first and foremost a weaving and crafts village, and to attract tradesmen advertisements in the *Aberdeen Journal* in February 1808 and February 1812 offered 'new built feu-houses … abundance of Firing … and commodious Croft Land'. The second advertisement offered employment to weavers.

Given that it was redesigned during the late eighteenth and early nineteenth century, geographers have often described the countryside in Buchan as a 'landscape of improvement'. Early nineteenth-century plans of Buchan such as that of Auchry by George Campbell Smith in 1830 highlight rectangular-shaped fields, substantial farms, shelter-belts of trees, and straight roads linking medium size villages. This view, taken in 1984 a short distance east of Cuminestown and looking towards Garmond, is of a rural landscape whose key features were created during the second half of the eighteenth century.

GARMOND, MONQUHITTER.

GAMMIE, PHOTO

Garmond evokes an almost timeless appearance in this photograph dating from about 1920. However, in reality the village was at the time experiencing significant depopulation. In 1871, 268 people lived there; in 1901 just 181. Sixty years later there were only 77 residents. It was once home to hand loom weavers, tailors, shoemakers and farm workers, occupations which either disappeared or declined in number as the nineteenth century progressed. The house facing the camera can still be seen at the southern edge of the village.

Left: Garmond School opened in August 1859 and was described as 'a very elegant structure, having four gothic windows, neat porch, a belfry, and tastefully laid out playground'. However, an aging population and fewer children led to calls by the Turriff Area School Committee to recommend closure of the thirteen-pupil school in 1952, with pupils being educated instead in Cuminestown. It remained open a further ten years thanks largely to the enterprising head teacher, Mrs Margaret Moir. When this photograph was taken in 1961 the roll stood at ten and during the following session it dropped to only seven a few weeks before the school closed on 8 January 1963. Just one member of the last class still lives in Garmond today, though several others work in the district.

Bottom left: In this charming photograph, John Fraser gives Santa, local farmer Angus Mitchell who is still wearing his farm boots, a present at the final Christmas party in Garmond School in 1962. Another occasion that captured the headlines in the local press a few years earlier was the staging of the pantomime, Dick Whittington, and with a cast of only eleven and very few boys to fill the parts, the *Turriff Advertiser* praised Mrs Moir, standing third from the left, for organising the event which took place in the parish church hall in Cuminestown.

Bottom right: In spite of its small population Garmond had a strong sense of community and an annual Highland Games day was held in the years between 1874 and the outbreak of the Second World War. The school was the venue for many social events including the ladies sewing class seen here about 1955. When the school closed the building became a community centre and hosted a varied programme of social events until 1995. More recently the old school building was advertised for sale by Aberdeenshire Council and when this author visited in February 2015 it was being converted into a house.

The village's licensed grocer's shop, which had a long history that can be traced back to early Victorian times, closed in 1963 and can be seen in this photograph, taken in 1984. It had been the only shop in the village since 1914. The photograph also highlights a number of gap sites created when old cottages were demolished. In the last ten years or so, younger families seeking a pleasant place to live have built new houses on many of the vacant sites.

The watercourse of the Burn of Monquhitter provided power for a number of mills on its banks and the sites of many of these can still be identified in local place names such as Mill of Pot, Waulkmill and Milton of Byth. Millfield, a dairy farm in the early twentieth century, is situated where the road from Cuminestown to New Byth crosses the burn. In 1870 the Ordnance Survey recorded a saw mill with its own water supply and a corn mill at Millfield. The meal mill was operated from 1907 by John William Milne until 1951. Milne served in the Boer War and at the Somme and was very active in the local community including the Garmond Games Committee and Monquhitter Bowling Club. This was the last water-powered mill in the district and remained in use until the late 1960s. After the mill closed the building was used for a short time to dry grain using electricity.

Upstream of Millfield Bridge was a pond with the water level controlled by a sluice as can be seen in this photograph taken in 1970. Today the sluice has gone and the water level in the pond is lower. However, the former mill lade is cleaned regularly and the farmer at Millfield Farm close by has thought of using the flow of water to generate electricity.

Mill of Byth lies within half a mile of the village and was a water-powered threshing mill. The Howe of Byth had a reputation for the superior quality of its grain produce and farmers from outlying areas would come in their carts for seed corn. Several generations of the Jack family were millers, the last member George Jack (1860–1938) retired from the mill in 1896 to take up the tenancy of the neighbouring farm of Milton of Byth. He was succeeded by James Harrison and his son John, probably photographed here, who had been millers at New Aberdour. John Harrison's death in 1909, when he was 44, led to his elderly father giving up the tenancy. Although long disused, the mill building is still standing. The mill lead which drew water from the burn several hundred yards upstream has however been filled in.

NEW BYTH

GAMMIE, PHOTO.

In 1899 the Rev. Thomas McWilliam published a history of New Byth to promote a bazaar to raise funds for the parish church at the top of the brae. Its title was *Sketch of a Quiet Buchan Parish* and the frontispiece is a view very similar to this taken from higher ground south of the village. New Byth certainly has the appearance of a fairly remote Buchan community situated some distance from the major towns of the district. It was also around eight to ten miles from the nearest railway stations at Maud and King Edward. A proposed Central Buchan line generated much public debate in 1893, but it was never built, much to the disappointment of people in the district. An isolated location and the area's dependence on agriculture no doubt contributed to New Byth recording the highest rate of depopulation among villages in Buchan between 1871 and 1901, when the population fell from 609 to only 351.

NEW BYTH.

Gammie, Photo.

Close to the village were the lotted lands rented from the Byth estate by around 40 tenants before the First World War. Between two and five acres were rented by most households and this was sufficient to keep a cow to produce milk for family use and for sale. The need to produce animal fodder influenced land utilisation with about half in grass and the remainder cropped on a five or six course rotation. This typically involved three years of grass, then oats, turnips and oats. Cows were housed in byres at the rear of the gardens that were accessible to the lanes and were driven out each day to pasture. Part-time farming supplemented family income and was a rewarding hobby that continued until about 50 years ago. Finally, the former distillery, another activity associated with local farming, is located in the trees on the left hand side of Bridge Street. After it closed in the mid-nineteenth century it became a grain and manure store.

During the eighteenth century worshippers in New Byth were faced with a return journey of almost 20 miles to attend King Edward Parish Church. In 1792 a former weaving shop on Bridge Street was converted into a Chapel of Ease, however by 1851 it was said to be in a ruinous condition and construction of a new church began later in the year near the junction of Main Street and Bridge Street. Designed by A. & W. Reid, architects, Elgin, it opened for worship on Sunday 27 June 1852 when a congregation of more than 700 people crammed in to hear the Rev. John Falconer preach 'a very impressive sermon from Rev.xxi. 22'. New Byth became a *quod sacra* parish in 1868, made up of sections of the parishes of King Edward, New Deer and Aberdour. Falling attendances led Buchan Presbytery in December 1992 to deem the kirk building 'no longer necessary' and limit spending to essential repairs. A formal union with Monquhitter church took place in 1995 and two years later the church building was sold and became an auction room but is currently empty. It is has been on the Buildings at Risk Register for nearly 20 years.

The Church of Scotland manse adjacent the church on Main Street was built at a cost of £300 in 1829, during the ministry of Gilbert Brown who went out to the Free Church in 1843. It continued to serve parishioners of the Church of Scotland until 1958 when Cuminestown and New Byth churches became a joint charge. The manse was sold by the Church two years later to Robert Murray who had just retired from farming at Byth House Home Farm and it became a private house known as Aldersyde.

THE MANSE, NEW BYTH.

Gammie, Photo.

SCHOOL, NEW BYTH

GAMMIE, PHOTO.

Land for the first school was provided by James Urquhart when he founded the village and this became known as the Charity School. Its successor, the building in the photograph, was begun in 1860 at the west end of the village in the area known as the 'Stackhill or Peat Stance'. When granting the site, the laird specified that 'the instruction … shall comprise at least … writing arithmetic geography scripture history and (in the case of girls) needlework'. An extension costing more than £2,000, much of it funded by a loan from the Public Works Loan Board, was completed in 1876 with the result that the school could now accommodate up to 180 pupils. However, it was replaced by a new school built in 1938 which closed on 1 July 2005 when the roll had fallen to only fifteen pupils.

This photograph of local school children possibly taken during their lunch break is a reminder that in late Victorian and Edwardian times most children grew up in large families. The owners of the merchant's shop on the right, William Anderson (1844–1922) and his wife Ann Duncan certainly contributed their share as they had eleven children though three girls died before they reached their teens. Anderson was born in Old Deer, and was a shoemaker and rural postman and bought the house and shop on the west side of Bridge Street in 1907. After his death, his daughters Annie and Isabella ran the business for a few years while a son, Edward, was still delivering the post in the 1940s.

Bridge Street, New Byth

Thatched single-storey cottages next to recently built two-storey houses often incorporating shop premises are a feature of photographs taken just before the First World War. During the difficult trading conditions of the inter-war period shops changed hands quite frequently. After the Anderson shop passed out of family ownership in 1929, it was named Elrick House by James John Watt who had farmed at Little Elrick, Old Deer Parish. It was bought by the Scottish Co-operative Wholesale Society in 1942. The Co-op remained in the village until 1957 when the house and shop were sold to James Craib McRobbie, a local lorry driver and his wife; however within two years it had closed and would not re-open again. Today the house has a forlorn appearance, the adjacent cottage feu is now a parking place, while a cottage on the opposite side of the street has also been demolished and has become a garden.

The advertisement in the *Aberdeen Journal* on 25 May 1763 which announced the founding of New Byth mentions that 'the Feuars will be accommodated with Firing, from a large Moss not a Quarter of a mile distant'. Each family were granted the right to cut two spades casting of peat from designated areas of moss. They were also allowed to take divots from the Hill of Tillymaud which was used to underline thatched roofs made of heather and broom. A four-wheeled cart heavily laden with peat can be seen in the street. Other details in this picture include a roadside tap installed as part of the village water scheme in 1874 where a man is filling a bottle and a lamp post which was erected as part of a voluntary lighting scheme project from 1902. The first cottage on the left was later demolished and the result can be seen on page 45.

The post office in New Byth, like the one in Cuminestown, has moved several times over the years. In the mid-nineteenth century it could be found on the east side of Main Street. Joseph Gibb was a shoemaker and postmaster for much of the Victorian period and in 1874 he moved to a single storey cottage halfway down the west side of Bridge Street. After his death in 1905 several of his daughters continued to run the post office business until 1944. When Jessie Gibb retired, the post office moved again this time uphill to the first house on the east side: 1–3 Bridge Street (pictured here). This was to become the last shop in the village and its closure along with postal services in 2006, following the death of local postmistress Margaret Whitecross, caused hardship for many elderly residents.

When James Godsman published his research on King Edward parish in 1952 he mentioned that many of the original two/three roomed thatched houses were still standing. These cottages in Main Street, photographed in 1975, were built to regulations requiring them to front directly on to the pavement. They make use of the local sandstone from the Cook and Delgaty quarries and originally had thatched roofs. In contrast, two-storey dwellings in New Byth and other villages in Buchan are mainly those built in the mid or late Victorian period, either to replace worn out housing or to create shops with living accommodation on the first floor.

The Square is situated at the northern end of Main Street. Typical single-storey cottages surround it on all sides while the countryside is only a short distance away, an arrangement that would have provided convenient access for animals being brought to fairs held here. A memorial to those who lost their lives in the First World War was erected on the west side of the Square and is situated near the cottage on the left hand side of the photograph. It was built of granite by Alexander Norrie of New Deer in memory of the 23 men from the parish who lost their lives in the conflict and was unveiled by Garden Alexander Duff of Hatton on Sunday 3 July 1921. Two days later the *Banffshire Journal* carried a very moving description of the memorial service at a packed parish church and the ceremony afterwards in the Square.

BYTH HOUSE.

GAMMIE, PHOTO.

Byth House was begun in the late sixteenth century and was extended in the early nineteenth century. Above the door on the right in the older part of the house there was a shield and the welcoming motto 'Velcum Freindis, 1593'. In the eighteenth century the house was owned by the Urquhart family. It was a traditional mansion, with a full range of public rooms on the ground floor, bedrooms with dressing rooms on the second floor and a servants' wing. Described by the Inland Revenue Survey around 1910 to be 'in fair condition but walls are done', the house along with the Home and Mains Farms were sold in 1925 to George Watt who had been a civil servant in Hong Kong. In 1928–29 he demolished much of the old mansion and built a new house on the same site. However, Watt's stay was short and in 1943–44 he sold the house and farmland while the tapestry and antique furniture went to dealers in Inverness and London. Watt and his wife moved to Aberdeen where he died in 1949.